The sun in the mirror

Poetry as Memoir

Nikki Powerhouse

The Sun in the Mirror © 2016 by Nikki Powerhouse

Cover Photo Credit: Shonda D. Nicholas

Publishing assistance provided by:
Tracey M. Lewis-Giggetts
NewSeason Books
www.newseasonbooks.com

All rights reserved. No part of this book may be reproduced in any form or by any means including electronic, mechanical or photocopying or stored in a retrieval system without permission in writing from the publisher except by a reviewer who may quote brief passages to be included in a review.

Manufactured and Printed in the United States of America

To my Mother/Ancestor who has transformed me through life and death: I AM because of you.

To my cousin, Karima Wadud/Ancestor: I chant the wisdom you gave to me daily, "No Meanness, No Fear, No Envy."

To You: Gratitude Overflows for your love, support, and encouragement.

Poetry is Therapy

A soul cleansing

A relentless breakthrough

I am a POET
Like the SUN
My therapy is WRITTEN
I am my own...

...HEALING

- Nikki Powerhouse

EARTH

In the Beginning

1.

I was pushed through a song
A child
    wrapped in hymns and hallelujahs

Both a savior for my mother and
    the light in my father's shadows
We would be the trinity
    Teacher
    Student
    Healer
Giving birth to each other
    Again
    Again
    Again
Until lessons were learned

Soul deep

2.

Dance Room

On Saturday mornings
My mother's bedroom held the brightest sun
I circled and giggled at the beat of pure freedom
The room felt both my mother's tears and my joy
A girl child who learned to see the world through

Rainbow colored eyes

3.

Daddy Soft Shoes

My father had wings
His arms outstretched
Poured into me all the freedom
he had to offer while we danced
We made magic
Combined the Sun and Thunder
Gliding words in the air

"Who loves you baby?"

The groove sounded so sweet
Girl innocence twirling in

"My D*addddddddddddy…*"

4.

No Daddy: *a haiku*

In the hood there is
no Santa, like no daddy
Just mom still trying.

FIRE
Eternal Flame

5.

Shine

When the moon feels heavy...
She denies herself her own Light
Settles for glimpses of shine
Hides behind dark spaces
Where her small becomes big enough

But her light can't hide at night
She was made to bring night its luster
A glow that makes shadows appear like
fluorescent angels

They remind her to invite the dark in
It is where she shines the brightest

6.

Fire Dance

Our dance is rhythmic
A call and response
Both spirit and flesh
unafraid as I nestle myself in your shadows
Your arms cloaking me in a prayer
Our dance becomes more like worship
A testimony of broken souls
Who carved freedom in their chest without
bleeding what they fear
We chose this dance to wail and shout like
mothers holding sons with bullets
bleeding white tee shirts
We have to keep moving
through the storms
The only way out is to
dance to your own

rhythm

7.

SHE (Burning Desire)

I loved her with a naked heart
A wide open soul
She made me feel feelings

foreign and free

Our time together was endless
Where nights turned into days
Between sun and moon
Made each moment
like a melody and base
playing around
Saturn rings

A muse that moved my senses
Where I heard her voice with eyes
And saw her beauty with hands
Her kiss dipped in honey and lemon

The bittersweet taste of love
I knew we would end when we began
But I wanted the page in my book
the one I wrote in my past life

8.

HER

Something about the way
she looks at me
Her commands
in a whisper
I'm made both
delicate and eager

9.

Skin: *a haiku*

Remember my touch
How your body disappears
Such a magician

10.

About Last Night...

You took my eyesight and made my vision sparkle
I couldn't craft the who or what
So my eyes tilted with my neck
So pleased by what I see
My eyes dripped in curiosity

I enjoyed the time, space and moment you took up
I felt my grown woman rise while my girl crush got tickled
I wanted to stay and see you brighter in your light
Beaming in all your
       "Brotha, you are so damn fine!"

What a treat to meet
 midnight at sunrise

11.

A Lover's Lie

Tonight we go nameless
Tangle in each other's loneliness
Let's pretend we will be forever
        in love

Forget the lust that brought our bodies here naked
This moment is magical
though a made up truth
        Our scars lie

12.

In Love w/HER

Never been so w i d e open
Where heart has a voice
and it speaks
     I Love You

In the morning, in afternoon, in evening
your absence is not missed
It's yearned for
My lips long to be greeted with chocolate kisses
While you wrap your arms around me twice
     First, my heart
     Then, my waist
It's always in that moment
I am reminded
This woman got me
     "Sweet girl!"

13.

My Little Girl and I

She sits in the corner
Staring with heat in her eyes
Her tears are flames
Black smoke trembles from her mouth

I want to save her but I can't hold the heat
The tears suffocate us both in

    shame and judgment

We reach for them,
he or she
to rescue us
But our stories have been burning for long nights
Making hissing sounds in cold rooms
while cradling the fear
of loving self boldly

We hear the whispers rattling

    "Get up!"
    "But where?"
    "Out of the story."

AND we knew once we left...

There was NO turning back.

wind

Everything must change

14.

Lonely Nights

She hates her image.
She thinks she is more beautiful
in secret
in dark rooms
with strangers

Her partners are often
as wounded as she
but neither notice
Such an entangled web
of self-inflicted
battle scars

So the night she calls romantic
is really just her chasing a fantasy
More like an addiction
to love
to hugs
to conversation
A room filled with screaming
empty moans while
her body is on mute
No passion
No connection
Just an escape
from herSelf.

15.

In Search: *a haiku*

She made no room for
Self love, but was wide open
Friends with benefits

16.

Night Walker

I played dress up
        Trying to paint pretty on
        But pretty never played fair in my skin

I twirled in my tall tales
In front of mirrors that cracked when
my reflection looked back

Years go by
The present carries past regrets
But the corner boy at night
makes me forget my dreams
        and I become addicted to nightmares

I wish I could pick up the pieces
that falls from my eyes
and craft a stronger
        Me.

17.

She Got Wings

The space we shared was distant and unfamiliar.
Our bloom is now dead leaves
scattered on crack grounds.
The journey no longer has legs to walk,
so we crawl our way out of future plans
with the memories and tears that cry from dry eyes.
This time I am not broken in pieces
No endless chatter.
Because the coldest summer has ended
and we are seasons
that just came to
a

    Fall...

18.

Crush No More: Part 1

I drove by the last place
I saw you...
        felt you...
                    looked into those exciting eyes
But honestly even then you felt distant
A memory fading into the present
Where the concrete
cracks
I was left standing on a fantasy
Hoping to return to yesterday's
illusion.

Crush No More: Part 2

I was reluctant to write about you
It felt so permanent
that your presence would soon be my past
A reality I'd rather think my way out of
        versus feel

But healing *is* feeling the absence of you
where I'm left alone with my first love
We make magic with tears and laughter
Finding the root and shedding the pain

Yes I wanted to paint love through the details
As we grew to learn ourselves
But everyone can't paint themselves raw like Frida

Twisted torso tangled in steel
We crashed and got quicker to the end

Now my future is my past
I AM my first love
      forever.

19.

My Mother is an Ancestor

My mother has unearthed the bottom of my soul
The very pit of ground zero
Getting up from this feels like the longest next step.

20.

Dimensions not Dementia

My mother is a Poet
That's the only way I can describe her
She shifts through memories
    Cotton candy,
    girl crushes,
    church altars,
Drugs houses
Locked away
Her past Is her NOW
She's chasing herself out of dark corners
Reaching for
    Mommy?
    Daddy?

They are not there

So she claws her way out
Only to return back
    cut deeply
    abandoned
    lost
    alone

Reaching for answers from tongues that
lie and laugh at her
    "Mommy come back! It's me, Babygirl!"
I'm screaming for her to return
For her to feel her flesh and bone with me

I watch her with lollipop eyes
Yet I hold her in crochet bundles of gospel hymns.
    Just like her mother did
Just like she
    remembers

21.

A Longer Memory

Memories flash
posing pretty and ugly.
Her mornings are often nights
where she screams against
windows, and cold white walls.
She remembers 12 years old
and the isolation chokes her.
Trying to vomit up her digust
from a memory that rots in her
little girl belly.
Someone is opening her door
shutting her out from safety.

22.

Feelings on Dementia: *a haiku*

I am my mother
She is me, we feel the same
This moment we scream

23.

Mommy Having a Good Day: *a haiku*

Her mind is present
I listen to her wisdom
It sounds like prayers

WATER

Rebirth

24.

Two Haikus in Motion

At rise she matters
She walks tall with Herstory
a poem in flight

Ancestors travel
beneath her feet with footprints
I am poetry

25.

Know My Worth: *a haiku*

Make love in color
With bodies beneath the sheets
Minds a cosmic play

26.

Ex-Lover, She Saved Me

My inner child misses being so
safe and beautiful
      with you

The way you invite her in
as if you knew her back then
When she learned how to hide
to keep secrets of the night
While they rattle throughout the day
her memories make hissing sounds

Shame and guilt was stored in her belly
but the sun bloomed on the inside
Every time you made her giggle, held her, or smiled at her
I never seen or felt her so safe before

She is playing again
in innocence and freedom

27.

Searching for LOVE

She is innocent
but hands that burn
leaves the little girl
in shame and guilt.

Her first game was played on her body
a playground with sticks and stone and
puddles of tears left on sliding boards.

I returned to get her but she runs...fast...then faster
Fear cracks in her eyes
She's trying to get away from herself
hating the image she sees

Tangled in riddles and lullabies
Her body broken in pieces
I, she, we are trying to collect stories buried under glass

But our hands are cut with insecurity, bleeding out
We blame you
Too big, I was too big
and my adult self hunts for big girl innocence

Where did it grow? I want to replant her
so only her innocence will bloom in yellow
and her blue tears water her roots
I, she, we find ourselves in freedom

Cradling in each other arms, our silence says I love you endlessly
We giggle, we smile
knowing it's safe to do

We be Girl and Woman
knowing it's safe to be…I AM

28.

THE MUSIC SHE HEARS IS
SILENCE
SHE KEEPS GOD ON
REPLAY.

29.

Amethyst Breath

I stand here unmeasurably tall
With arms extended in grace
While hands make rhythmic motion back and forth
The body lied cold
Hand held memories being a once crocheted bundle in her arms
I wrapped my mother in
suns and moons
Sent her flying
ascending on a wing of amethyst breath
All around her is stars and rings
A prayer in motion
Her silence echoes through deep waters
I bathe there
Return there
To be reborn
She gives me life
In each deep breath
I surrender in her love
My love
Our love
A gift
unto one another

30.

Haiku Again

Extraordinary
She is a whisper that sings
In courage and strength.

31.

Dance Divinity 1

Dance with my shadows
Twirling in my brightest self
Darkness is my light.

Dance Divinity 2

When she dances...
something inside bursts
in yellow
The sun at night
enjoys
her
own

32.

Mood swings

I DO NOT FEEL LIKE WRITING
Trying to burn the words into perfection
Pushing through pain
While my breath kicks through screams

NOOOOO
I'd rather not unearth my fragile heart
Drag it through memories cloaked in
scars and fear

I'll just sit in silence
and let words become

TEARS.

33.

Meditation

I AM awake
I lie in silence
Cocoon in its safety
My breath in the air plays
like piano keys
a melody of peace

I AM connected,
embracing the calm
No need to run

I AM safe now
in my
stillness

34.

Tears

Today I allowed tears to fall
No particular reason
But just to let them fall

35.

To My Inner child

You wanted to be grown so fast
Chasing want seemed to be your ticket out
But there's no out if you're skipping over your innocence
Trying to find pretty between sheets that left you ugly
Oh no, my precious
No need to speed up tomorrow
Savor the flavor of your sweetness
Indulge yourself with love letters
Bloom from your image
Your smile is enough validation
From the seeds you plant
color rooms with laughter
Make up your face with magic
Dress up in magnificence
Tell stories that begin with I AM in front of mirrors that glow back at you
You're only but a child once
Embrace your Magic

36.

Mama Pauline

I lay in my mother's arms
Baptized in her grace
My tears meet God in her heart
I'm loved fiercely.

37.

Letting Go

I woke up to
MORE
so I let go of
less.

38.

Gentle

He embraced me with his eyes
Bringing me closer to his heart
Awakening my innocence
with his rhythmic whisper
      "I love you woman."
Sparkle.

39.

Keep Going

To get to the end of
silence
means I got through the
screams
along the way

Reach out to Nikki Powerhouse:

Website
www.NikkiPowerhouse.com

Follow @NikkiPowerhouse on
FB/Twitter/Instagram

Made in the USA
Middletown, DE
11 September 2016